STORIES JESUS TOLD

Tim Dowley

Illustrations by Gordon King

Bible Society

THE STORY OF THE SOWER

One day Jesus was telling people a story.

Listen! There was once a farmer who went out to sow seed.
As he sowed, some of his seed fell on the path. Birds flew down and gobbled up that seed.
Some seed fell in stony places.
That seed soon sprang up, because there wasn't much earth.
But when the sun shone the shoots withered away.
Some seed fell in the middle of thorns.
When the thorns grew up, they choked the plants that grew from that seed.
But some of the farmer's seed fell on good ground.
It sprang up with strong, green shoots.
When harvest came, that seed produced golden grain for the farmer.

What does it mean?
Everyone enjoyed listening to Jesus' story.
But when the crowds had gone home, Jesus' closest friends asked:
"What does this story about the sower mean?"
So Jesus said: "People who listen to what God says to them, and then do what he tells them, are like good ground that produces plenty of good crops."

THE SON WHO CAME BACK

The people gathered around Jesus to listen to another of his stories.
When they had all sat down, he began.

There lived a rich farmer who had two sons.
Both sons worked on the farm with him.
If the father died, both sons would get part of the farm;
but the elder son would get the bigger share.

"Give me my share"
As he grew up, the younger son began to get restless.
One day he went to his father.
"Father," he said, "please give me my share now.
I want to set out into the world and try to make my fortune."
His father was sad to let him go, but he agreed to do as his son asked.
Soon the younger son left home, carrying with him the money his father had given him.

A good time
When the younger son reached a city, he began spending his money and soon made plenty of new friends.
He invited them to parties and dances and bought them wine and food and expensive presents.
For a while he had a wonderful time.

Hungry!

But it wasn't long before the younger son had used up the money his father had given him.

And — what a nasty surprise! — his new friends soon disappeared.

They no longer wanted to know him, now that he had no money.

Soon the younger son didn't have enough to eat.

He began to look for work.

But even work wasn't easy to find.

Feeding pigs

At last he found himself a job, feeding the pigs for a farmer.

As he watched the pigs guzzling at the trough, his own stomach rumbled with hunger.

He thought sadly of his far-off home, where there was always plenty to eat.

A plan

"What a fool I have been!" he said to himself.

"At home I always had enough to eat; and my family loved me.

Here I'm hungry and lonely."

Then he had an idea.

"I'll go back home," he decided.

"Of course I can't expect father to take me back as his son.

But I'll tell him that I've done wrong.

At least he might take me in as a servant."

Journeying home

So the young son travelled slowly home.
But when he was still a long way off, his father saw him.
He had never forgotten his son; every day he thought of him, and wondered what he was doing.

Father's greeting

As soon as he saw his son coming, the father raced off down the road to meet him.

When he met him, he hugged him hard.

Once he'd got back his breath, the young man said: "Father, I have done wrong.

I don't deserve to be called your son."

But his father paid no attention.

He shouted to his servants: "Go bring my best coat! Bring him some shoes!

Get my gold ring!

My son who was lost is found."

Then he had another thought.

"Kill the calf," he called.

"We'll have a great party to celebrate!"

The party

Soon the party was going.

Just then the older brother, who had been working all day in the fields, came home.

When he heard all the noise, he asked what was going on.

"There's a party," said a servant.

"A party?" said the elder son. "Whose party?"

"It's for your brother.

He's come back!"

The angry son

Then the elder son was angry.

He stormed up to his father.

"I've stayed at home all these years, working for you, day in and day out.

You've never given me a party!
Now this good-for-nothing turns up again, and you kill
the calf and have a great feast.
It's not fair!"
But the old man said: "All I have is yours.
But we must celebrate, because my lost son has come
home."

And Jesus said, "God rejoices when anyone turns to
him and says they have done wrong."

THE GOOD NEIGHBOUR

Another time Jesus told the people this story about a man who was robbed.

Once a traveller set out to walk from Jerusalem to Jericho.
The road was very lonely and went between rocky hills.
As the traveller was going through the hills, robbers surprised him.
They beat him up, stole his money and clothes, and left him for dead.

A priest passes

A little later a man from the Temple came past.
But when he saw the body of the traveller on the road,
he simply crossed the road and walked a bit faster.
A little later still another man from the Temple came by.
When he saw the body of the traveller lying in the road,
he too crossed the road and walked a bit faster.

The Samaritan stops

Then a man from Samaria came down the road.
Now Jews and Samaritans hate each other.
So that man wasn't likely to help.
But when the Samaritan saw the traveller lying in the road, he was sorry for him.
So he got down from his donkey and washed the man's wounds.
Then he poured oil and wine on his wounds to soothe them.
Finally he bandaged up the traveller's wounds.
Then he lifted him up onto his donkey and set off gently down the road.

At the hotel

After a time they reached an hotel.
The Samaritan helped the traveller inside.
He said to the hotel-keeper:
"I found this wounded traveller on the road.
Care for him until he feels well again."
And he paid the hotel-keeper two silver coins.
"Look after him well," he said.
"I'll be back in a few days.
So if you need more money,
I'll pay you then."

Who is the good neighbour?

Then Jesus turned to the people listening.
"Which man do you think acted like a good neighbour?"
And of course they all knew the answer.
So Jesus said: "You must do the same."

THE LOST SHEEP

Jesus told his followers this story about a lost sheep.

Once there was a shepherd who had a hundred sheep.
Each day he took his sheep out into the countryside to
find grass to nibble and water to drink.
Each night he led them back to the sheep-fold, so they
would sleep safe from wild animals.

Only ninety-nine!

One night when he counted his sheep there were only ninety-nine.

So he counted again to make sure.

Still only ninety-nine!

The shepherd was worried.

He locked the ninety-nine safely in the sheep-fold, and set out into the night to find the lost sheep.

He climbed hills, crawled over rocks, and searched the river's edge.

He was scratched by thorns and felt very cold in the night air.

Then he heard something crying softly.

Found!

Soon he had found the lost sheep, caught in some thorns.

He pulled it out and laid it gently on his strong shoulders.

The shepherd walked home tired but happy.

Celebrations!

He called to his friends: "Come and celebrate! The lost sheep is found!"

And Jesus said, "God is just as happy when somebody turns to him and says he is sorry for doing wrong."

A STRONG HOUSE

Jesus had another story for the crowd.

Once two men decided to build themselves houses.
One man was wise; before he started, he looked for solid rock to build on.
When he had found a rocky place, he built his house and moved in.
When winter came, the winds blew against the house, and the rain beat down on it.
But the wise man's house didn't fall, because it was built on the rock.

The foolish man
But the other man was foolish; he couldn't be bothered to find a rocky place to build.
He found a nice stretch of sand and built his house there.
But when winter came, the winds blew against the house and the rain beat on it, until suddenly one night his house fell down BANG!

Then Jesus said: "People who listen to me, and then go away and do as I say, are like the wise man.
They are building their lives on rock.
But if you don't obey my words, you are like the foolish man who built his house on sand!"

For parents and teachers

You can find these stories in your Bible.

The story of the sower: Matthew 13.1-23
The son who came back: Luke 15.11-32
The good neighbour: Luke 10.25-37
The lost sheep: Luke 15.1-7
A strong house: Matthew 7.24-27